sur

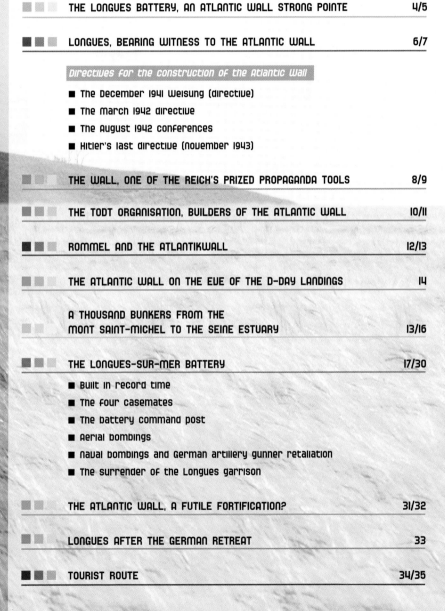

GW01003262

The Longues battery, An Atlantic Wall strong point

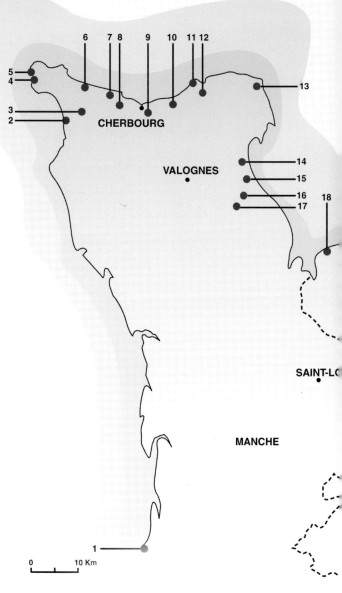

The German coastal artillery battery at Longues-sur-Mer, located on the Calvados coastline, is an excellent example of an Atlantic Wall strong point. The Longues bunkers are not unique and, today, the Normandy coastline still hosts the more or less preserved relics of thirty or so of the Wehrmacht's artillery batteries between the Mont Saint-Michel and Le Havre. However, the German battery at Longues is particularly noteworthy since it is the only one to have preserved its guns. By some mysterious miracle, it managed to escape the fervent salvage operations by post-war scrap merchants.

▦ Map of German coastal artillery batteries on the lower Normandy coastline in June 1944.

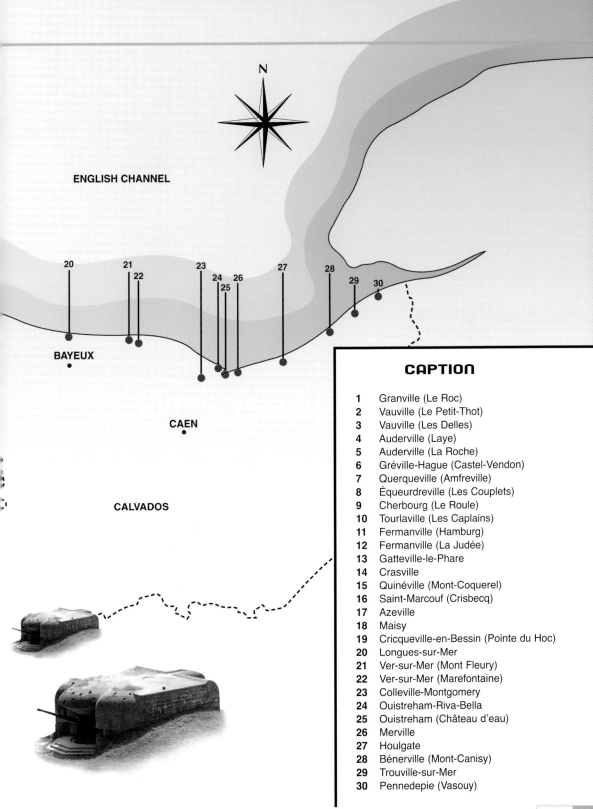

N

ENGLISH CHANNEL

20 21   23   27   28
    22   24 26   29 30
            25

BAYEUX

CAEN

CALVADOS

CAPTION

1	Granville (Le Roc)
2	Vauville (Le Petit-Thot)
3	Vauville (Les Delles)
4	Auderville (Laye)
5	Auderville (La Roche)
6	Gréville-Hague (Castel-Vendon)
7	Querqueville (Amfreville)
8	Équeurdreville (Les Couplets)
9	Cherbourg (Le Roule)
10	Tourlaville (Les Caplains)
11	Fermanville (Hamburg)
12	Fermanville (La Judée)
13	Gatteville-le-Phare
14	Crasville
15	Quinéville (Mont-Coquerel)
16	Saint-Marcouf (Crisbecq)
17	Azeville
18	Maisy
19	Cricqueville-en-Bessin (Pointe du Hoc)
20	Longues-sur-Mer
21	Ver-sur-Mer (Mont Fleury)
22	Ver-sur-Mer (Marefontaine)
23	Colleville-Montgomery
24	Ouistreham-Riva-Bella
25	Ouistreham (Château d'eau)
26	Merville
27	Houlgate
28	Bénerville (Mont-Canisy)
29	Trouville-sur-Mer
30	Pennedepie (Vasouy)

Construction of the Longues coastal artillery battery began in the autumn of 1943 and was undertaken by the German Navy. The construction of the Atlantic Wall had, in fact, begun far earlier.

DIRECTIVES FOR THE CONSTRUCTION OF THE ATLANTIC WALL

The decision to build a fortified line on the Western European coastline, from the North Cape to the Spanish border? was made by Hitler on the 14th of December 1941, immediately after the United States entered into World War II.

THE DECEMBER 1941 WEISUNG (DIRECTIVE)

In anticipation of the threat of an Anglo-American landing operation behind the German lines, whilst the best part of the Wehrmacht was posted on the Russian front, Hitler announced his intention to build a fortified line along the Western European coastline. By its mere presence, and its potential danger to any assailant, the rampart was intended to discourage the Western Allies from any attempted landing operation. The December 1941 directive set the priorities that were to be respected in order to achieve coastal defence: according to the dictator, the seafront between Antwerp and Le Havre was the most vulnerable, followed by the Atlantic coast, the

Brittany and Normandy coasts and, finally, the Dutch and Jutland coast.

THE MARCH 1942 DIRECTIVE

The multiplication of British raids on the Norwegian and French coasts together with the success of the first Soviet counter-offensive (winter of 1941-1942) which had forced the German high command to retreat from the Channel coastline, had somewhat disquieted Berlin.

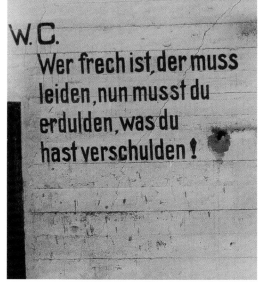

■ Inscription on the wall of the "Todt" long range coastal artillery battery at Longues. The rather arrogant message which is directly addressed to Winston Churchill reads as follows, "Whoever is insolent, must suffer, you will now pay for your ill deeds".

Hitler also published a second instruction on the 23rd of March 1942 concerning the protection of the Western European shoreline. Whereas the December directive had been a general text outlining the necessity to defend the European coasts, the March 1942 directive addressed the problem of the organisation of coastal defence and entrusted the immense coastal fortification programme to the Todt Organisation.

THE AUGUST 1942 CONFERENCES

A few days before the Dieppe raid (19th of August) and immediately after the Canadian operation, Hitler reconsidered the question of coastal fortification during a series of conferences. Whilst the Wehrmacht was at a virtual standstill on the banks of the Volga, the dictator was well aware that a landing operation on the Channel coast would herald a major threat and he estimated that some 15,000 bunkers needed to be built along the coast, armed by 300,000 soldiers to ensure coastal surveillance. He finally ordered the Todt Organisation to accelerate building work and to finalise the construction of the fortified line by the 1st of May 1943.

HITLER'S LAST DIRECTIVE (NOVEMBER 1943)

In the autumn of 1943, Field Marshal Von Rundstedt, Supreme Commander West, drew an alarming portrait of the Wehrmacht's position on the Western front in a report sent to the dictator. Over and above their insufficient numbers, their poor quality and inadequate armaments, Von Rundstedt insisted on the delays encountered in the execution of the coastal fortification programme.

■ *Gegen Engeland (against England), which should normally have been written "England", however the pronunciation tempo required the deformation to "Engeland". These two words are taken from a famous military march sung by Luftwaffe troops in 1940. This painting, on the wall of the "Todt" long range coastal artillery battery at Longues in the North of France, depicts the different military forces required to invade Great Britain.*

Upon this distress signal, Hitler announced, in his final directive (on the 3rd of November) a whole series of measures concerning the Atlantic Wall aimed at reinforcing the defensive capacities of the armed forces guarding the coastline. To prove his conviction that the Western front should no longer be neglected to profit the Russian front, the dictator appointed the popular Field Marshal Rommel to inspect fortifications and to command the battle against allied invasion. To lead this mission that was of capital importance for Germany's fate, Hitler appointed Rommel to the post of Commander of Army Group B which reunited the 15th and 7th Army, together comprising more than half a million men.

THE WALL, ONE OF THE REICH'S PRIZED PROPAGANDA TOOLS

Presented as a formidable and armoured concrete barrage, riddled with large machine guns, the Wall was subject to vast propaganda aimed, not only at exerting a reassuring influence on the German civilian population, but also at intimidating the Anglo-Saxon population. As the subject of a great number of articles, photo reports, newsreels and radio programmes, the Wall, which was Hitler's pride an joy, had also become the destination of Hungarian, Bulgarian, Rumanian, Italian, Finish, Turkish, Spanish and even Japanese military missions to the Western front. As already mentioned, the Wall was the subject of many an article and the Todt Organisation was endowed with a highly active propaganda service which provided a multitude of technical details on sheets handed out to journalists. Here is an example of an article published in the magazine "L'Illustration" in May 1943.

"The wall is even more extraordinary than we ever imagined. The audacity of its conception and the quantity of work engaged in its execution are barely believable. The only comparison to be found in history is the great wall erected to fight the Mongol invasions in the North of China, along a border of some 3,000 km. European coastal protection stretches from the North Cape to the Pyrenean Mountains. Across the 2,700 km of our coastline, there is no spot left unprepared to retaliate against a powerful attack. Immediately after the armistice, the Todt Organisation began fortification of coastal zones along the Channel and the installation of long range batteries firing occasionally towards Dover. It then set to the construction of submarine bases. In February 1942, inspired by experience from the Westwall (or Siegfried line) construction, the Fuhrer ordered the edification of the Atlantic rampart. The former, covering an 850 km front and including some 22,000 concrete bunkers, had been rapidly built in advantageous peacetime circumstances, whereas the Atlantikwall was to be built in the midst of the war, despite enemy airborne attacks and the depletion of efficient transport...

Six thousand permanent elements and five thousand mobile elements, very high calibre guns fixed onto railway lines and rapid-fire anti-tank guns are all ready for action. Hundreds of thousands of labourers of various nationalities have been employed. Germans provided the teams' framework and represented 10% of the total labour force. As and when the young workers were called to arms, veterans stepped in to replace them. Team leaders commanded from 50 to 200 non-German labourers. The Todt Organisation has in its possession very many foreign foremen. Members of the Legion of French Volunteers (LVF) having distinguished themselves on the Eastern front masterfully managed these teams of French workers, many of whom had already worked on the construction of the Maginot Line. Two hundred thousand Frenchmen, among whom many volunteers, have worked on the Atlantic rampart".

The true figures were, of course, inferior to those mentioned in this article aimed at brainwashing. According to the Ob. West (the German supreme command in the Western front), at the end of 1943, there were, in fact, 2,692 pieces of artillery of a calibre superior to 7.5 cm on the Atlantic Wall.

■ Propaganda poster in Dutch exalting the strength of the Atlantic Wall. The coastal fortification is presented on this poster as a continuous and impenetrable line. The very concise text simply announces that 1943 will not be like 1918, the year on which the Second Reich was forced to sign armistice.

■ On the left, we can distinguish Field Marshal Gerd von Rundstedt, supreme commander of the Western front as from March 1942. He was in charge of supervising the Atlantic Wall construction.

■ Sangatte, the most powerful of the Atlantic Wall coastal artillery batteries. This 40.6 cm (16 inch) calibre gun, large enough for a man to slide inside, fired across-Channel as far as the English coast, which at this location, was some 30 km away. Built in 1941, each of the three German artillery bunkers comprised 17,000 m³ of armoured concrete, measured approximately 50 m long and 17 m high. The firing chamber was situated on the ground floor, the sleeping quarters on the intermediate floor and, on the upper floor, water and fuel supplies as well as electric generators. All of the Todt Organisation's propaganda films included shots of this prestigious battery.

THE TODT ORGANISATION, BUILDERS OF THE ATLANTIC WALL

■ Battery of concrete mixers on a major building site on the Cotentin Peninsula. The Todt Organisation always sought building companies with high-performance equipment.

reated by Hitler and named after the engineer Fritz Todt, the Todt Organisation's main mission was to provide work for Germany's abundant unemployed in 1933. The Todt Organisation's first major project was the construction of German motorways. Then came the construction of what was to be known as the Westwall on the Reich's Western border. Following France's defeat, the organisation run by Fritz Todt abandoned the Siegfried Line to concentrate its efforts on the Pas-de-Calais coastline, building, within a few weeks, several major heavy artillery batteries aimed at protecting the fleets that were to land on British soil. The following year, the German construction agency accomplished another great feat by building five submarine bases on the French coastline (Brest, Lorient, La Pallice, Saint-Nazaire and Bordeaux).

In the spring of 1942, whilst continuing construction work on the submarine bases and on Luftwaffe airfields, the Todt Organisation's major task became the construction of the Atlantic Wall on the Western European coastline (Netherlands, Belgium and France). At the end of 1942, the French Mediterranean coast was added to the already demanding construction programme. The Todt Organisation employed the Reich's leading public works companies to ensure the construction of the fortified line. Unable to guarantee, alone, the completion of the European coastal defence within the given time limits, the German companies sub-contracted part of the work to eminent French public works companies.

According to an allied report based on post-

■ Amfreville (near Cherbourg) – Firing command post of a long-range (17 cm) coatal artillery battery.

■ Construction of a casemate at La Hague to the west of Cherbourg.

war declarations from ex-executives from the Todt Organisation, there were, in 1944, between one thousand and one thousand five hundred French companies employed by the German organisation. Among these entrepreneurs, there were a number of volunteers eager to take part in the Nazi cause and

to earn large sums of easy money. It is estimated that they represented approximately a third of the total French workforce.

Contrary to these volunteers, the companies from the second group forming the majority of the French workforce were requisitioned; in other words, they had never sought to anticipate the enemy's demands. They agreed to be requisitioned in order to save their equipment and their workforce. Depending on the personality of their leaders, these requisitioned companies could become an excellent refuge for refractories or even information

agencies for the allies. Up to the spring of 1942, the Todt Organisation's numbers were relatively mediocre (approximately 70,000 labourers). There were insufficient volunteers, and the occupier exerted pressure on the Vichy government to obtain further manpower. Thanks to an active recruitment campaign, Vichy provided around 200,000 men: French and colonials (Africans and Indochinese). However, numbers remained insufficient, and the Todt Organisation had so-called volunteer workers, as well as forced labourers, brought from occupied Eastern territories (Poland, Czechoslovakia, Russia…). On the eve of the D-Day landings, the Todt Organisation had some 300,000 workers at its disposal.

■ Different types of radar installed along the Atlantic Wall. Certain devices were specialised in long-range aerial surveillance, others were in charge of informing the Flak (anti-aircraft defence).

■ ■ ■ ROMMEL AND THE ATLANTIC WALL

Although his reign was brief, Rommel had a significant influence on the coastal defence system. Contrary to Field Marshal von Rundstedt who, after the war, qualified the wall as a monstrous bluff, Rommel had faith in the concrete line's efficacy and would do everything in his power to reinforce it.

■ In the centre Rommel, on the left General Marcks, Commander of the 84th Army Corps (headquarters in Saint-Lô), and on the extreme right, General Speidel, Rommel's Chief of Staff.

■ Omaha Beach – Tobruk surmounted by an old tank turret.

The ex-Afrika Korps commander was undoubtedly the Atlantic Wall's best advocate. He accomplished the incredible feat of transforming this succession of concrete forts separated by stretches of uncovered coastline, into a continuous defensive cordon, whilst giving a certain depth to the entire blockade. He reduced the number of major construction sites, which involved lengthy delays and required substantial material supplies and abundant manpower, multiplying, on the contrary, the number of small defensive installations, combat emplacements, trenches, false battery positions to draw enemy fire, anti-tank ditches and walls as well as concrete bunkers (or tobruks) sheltering flame-throwers or surmounted by an old French tank turret.

In the same endeavour to block potential assailants on the shore, Rommel had thousands of obstacles driven into the sand. Comprised of wooden or concrete stakes, heavy metallic barriers, tetrahedrons, chevaux-de-frise, hedgehogs assembled with portions of railway track, hundreds of thousands of obstacles aimed at tearing open the hulls of landing barges, were arranged in such a manner that they would be effective against any landing attempt, be it by low or by high tide.

■ Rommel offered an accordeon to the troops who paid the best attention to his instructions, for ensuring the defence of the coast against invasion.

■ Field Marshal Rommel with soldiers from the Wehrmacht close to the Channel shores.

As from January 1944, he gave the order to multiply minefields further inland. Failing to reach his objective of one mine per square metre, Rommel did, however, have some five millions mines set between January and June 1944. In the same manner, he did not hesitate to open the locks protecting many marshlands and lowlands against fresh or seawater inundation, hence provoking the flooding of over 25,000 hectares in France alone. And finally, he ordered for strips of forest to be cut down and for planes to be cleared of trees in order to plant tens of thousands of wooden stakes throughout any meadows potentially suitable for major airborne operations or for landing gliders. All of this work, feverishly and efficiently executed in the space of only a few months, rendered the Wall an increasingly formidable obstacle. Over and

above this work, the Todt Organisation, in a new lease of life, had managed to erect, from January to June 1944, thousands of small defensive installations bringing the total number of Atlantic Wall elements to around ten thousand. The Todt Organisation's performance was all the more remarkable since, at the same time, it undertook the repair of damage caused by allied bombardments to engineering structures and railway lines as well as the construction of large bunkers aimed at launching secret weapons.

■ Firing emplacement on the Atlantikwall.

THE ATLANTIC WALL ON THE EVE OF THE D-DAY LANDINGS

In accordance with Hitler's directive n° 51, the Western front was strengthened by a number of human and material reinforcements, whilst Rommel endeavoured to confer continuity and depth to the fortification line. From autumn 1943 to spring 1944, the number of divisions under the orders of Von Rundstedt increased from thirty-eight to fifty-nine, among whom a number of Panzerdivisionen (armoured divisions).

DER SCHILD EUROPAS

■ The caption talks of the European shield. This caricature, published in one of the Reich's newspapers in 1943, perfectly sums up the German defence strategy set up along the Western European coastline: the shield (the Atlantic Wall) against which Churchill would collide, and aimed at hindering the assailants' progression along the coast, and the sword (the Wehrmacht and its armoured divisions whose task was to counterattack and send the allies back into the sea).

They constituted the striking force that was to throw the Allies back into the sea.

Within the German defence strategy, the Wall was only aimed at slowing down allied progression. Similar progress was achieved with regard to the firing power of the Atlantic Wall fortifications. In June 1944, there were over three thousand pieces of artillery ranging from 7.5 cm to 40.6 cm, to which we can add thousands of anti-tank guns, machine guns and anti-aircraft artillery.

In short, the coastal defence system was far from being an illusion. However, the Wall, as far as the number of guns or the quality of troops was concerned, was not quite what Goebbels' propaganda would have us believe with his slogan, "In Dieppe, they held out for six hours, the next time, they won't last an hour".

A THOUSAND BUNKERS FROM THE MONT SAINT-MICHEL TO THE SEINE ESTUARY

Saint-Marcouf (or Crisbecq), on the Cotentin Peninsula. This heavy artillery battery equipped with 20.3cm Skoda guns was to be massively bombarded before the 6th of June. Contrary to the Longues battery, the Saint-Marcouf garrison was to withstand the American assaults over several days before retreating to the Cherbourg fortress.

Without a doubt, the most striking characteristic of the German coastal fortification is its uniformity and its monotony, stemming from the excessive standardisation of its different elements; the only method enabling the Todt Organisation to guarantee the rapid progress of construction sites. Mass produced, repetitive, anonymous, devoid of fantasy, damp, unhealthy and designed to kill, the concrete and iron cubes were all alike, as much in terms of the materials used, the shape, the colour, the position of openings, the entrance defence system, the construction depth as in terms of the interior fittings (armoured doors, ventilation, electricity, telephone...). One can however distinguish among these concrete monsters, nowadays either sand-ridden or overturned on the shore, the ones that were known as active (those housing a weapon), the very varied shelter category

Saint-Pierre-Eglise (Cotentin) German radionavigation station.

A THOUSAND BUNKERS FROM
THE MONT SAINT-MICHEL TO THE SEINE ESTUARY

■ Open artillery battery on a circular concrete platform (Cherbourg sector).

In June 1944, from the Mont Saint-Michel to the Seine Estuary, almost one thousand concrete fortifications adorned the 450 kms of coastline, to which should be added just as many brick, concrete block or sheet-metal constructions as well as camps.

Despite their great physical resemblance, each and every bunker played a specific role in the coastal defence plan. The Germans having no military fleet capable of establishing a sufficiently solid barrier at sea, the long range artillery batteries, those daunting concrete fortifications built close to the shore, were assigned the task of ensuring the long distance defence of the Festung Europa (Fortress Europe).

(observation, command, transmission, ammunition holds, garages), underground shelters (workshops, storerooms, depositories, hospitals) as well as the special constructions (radar or radionavigation stations, and V1 or V2 secret weapon launch bases).
We can add to the above list the submarine bases sheltering speed boats at Cherbourg and, in particular, at Le Havre.

The numerous smaller constructions housing one piece of low calibre artillery, a machine gun, a grenade launcher or a tank turret, were to ensure the defence of the nearby coast (fighting against landing barges, tanks or assailants attempting to set foot on the coast).

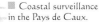

■ Coastal surveillance in the Pays de Caux.

THE LONGUES-SUR-MER BATTERY

In the Seine Bay (between Barfleur point and the Seine estuary), there were twenty artillery batteries in June 1944, representing a good hundred guns. Apart from the batteries in Auderville (20.3 cm), Amfreville (17 cm), Fermanville (Hamburg 24 cm), La Pernelle (17 cm) and Saint-Marcouf (which the Americans called Crisbecq) armed with four huge 21 cm Czech guns, the majority of the Seine Bay artillery positions were equipped with weapons of French origin, with an average calibre of 15.5 cm.

Just to the North of Bayeux, only 6 kilometres from Arromanches, more or less in the centre of the profound re-entrant that constitutes the Seine Bay, the Longues battery is one of the most unwonted of the sites forming the landing zone. Built on a treeless plateau, on the summit of picturesque cliff-top, the position comprises four 15 cm calibre guns and, in the foreground, just before the cliff-edge, stands an observation post. Placed within casemates (bunkers endowed with a large window known as a gun port to enable firing), the guns, whose mission was to prevent enemy fleets from approaching the shore, were capable of firing a target crossing at some twenty kilometres out to sea.

BUILT IN RECORD TIME

Just like all the other major construction works forming the Atlantic Wall, but with the added curiosity of being situated right in the centre of the future Anglo-American landing zone, the Longues guns were the target of several aerial reconnaissance missions. For such hazardous investigative missions, the British used very rapid planes, capable of flying at high altitude (30,000 ft), such as Spitfires or Mosquitos equipped with a narrow-angle lens camera. Thanks to periodical coverage of the coast, the Allied Staff was able to keep up with the Atlantic Wall's advancement.

The two following pictures, taken by the RAF just before the D-Day landings, are an excellent example of the quantity and the accuracy of information offered by aerial reconnaissance, which proved to be the primary source of information to the allies during the final conflict.

■ View of casemates in the distance

THE LONGUES-SUR-MER BATTERY

On the aerial photograph dated the 2nd of March 1944, we can distinguish, in the lower right-hand corner, a few of the village houses surrounded by planted fields. Between the village and the cliff-top that overhangs the Channel, it is clear that, three months before Operation Overlord was launched, the construction of the coastal artillery battery had barely commenced.

Three roads had been traced across the parcels of cultivated land for public works vehicles and lorries. Two major excavation sites, both destined to house a casemate, are perfectly visible on the road parallel to the coast. Other construction sites, of a smaller scale apart from the firing command post on the cliff-top, can also be seen on this exceptionally clear picture.

On the second photograph, taken on the 22nd of May at low tide, the Longues construction site had taken on a totally new look. Roads, large and small concrete constructions and zigzagging networks of

■ Aerial photograph of the Longues site, dated 2nd March 1944

trenches had proliferated. The artillery position now resembles a genuine little fortress.

With a magnifying glass, one can clearly distinguish the four firing casemates hidden, as was the Todt Organisation's custom, under huge camouflage nets hung over wooden stakes.

It would appear that only German companies were involved in the construction of Longues, which was originally a Kriegs-marine coastal artillery battery which was to be retroceded to the Land Army shortly before the D-day landings. The German firms benefited from manpower comprising prisoners of war and forced labourers from Eastern Europe.

Comparison between the two pictures brings to light the extraordinary efficacy of the Todt Organisation, made possible by the excessive standardisation of the concrete elements and the abundant, unrelenting and totally free manpower.

■ Aerial photograph of the Longues site, dated 22nd May 1944

■ Longues – View of the casemates. The tiered concrete visor aimed at protecting the gun port against a direct hit from the high sea is clearly visible.

THE FOUR CASEMATES

Huge concrete cubes each of them sheltering a piece of artillery, the casemates measured approximately fifteen metres long, ten metres large and a slightly over six metres high. The construction of each cube required approximately 600 m³ of concrete and around 4 tons of metallic reinforcements. The roofing slab and the walls are just over two metres thick. Such protection rendered the Longues guns practically invulnerable to aerial bombings. The casemates were built on a substantial concrete foundation in order to avoid tipping in the case of a projectile exploding close to an abutment. Each casemate consisted of a firing chamber housing the artillery and, to the rear, two smaller chambers for storing ammunition. At Longues,

there was a trench just under the gun for storing used cartridge cases. Above the gun, large ducts drew the noxious gases that accumulated in the chamber after a few rounds had been fired. With their large curved contours, the Longues casemates are partly concealed by a deep layer of earth forming a sloping plane supported on either side of the firing chamber by the abutments. These heaps of earth were also intended to serve as an anti-spalling layer, in other words, they were to absorb the shockwaves of projectiles exploding at the foot of the casemate. The edges of the concrete roof were decked with iron hooks to attach the camouflage netting. Over two

metres thick, the heavy concrete roof extends over the gun in a semi-circular visor built in tiers in order to protect the artillery against falling projectiles.

Facing the sea, each of the Longues casemates had a firing range of approximately 100 degrees horizontally and 40 degrees vertically.

The gashes cut into the base of the abutments at either side of the gun were aimed

■ Longues – Casemate avec son canon – Les trous dans le béton étaient destinés au camouflage (mottes d'herbe, fleurs).

at increasing the firing range by a few degrees to the extreme east and west.

In 1944, there were several underground shelters close to the casemates serving as accommodation quarters for artillerymen as well as ammunition holds. The whole site was protected by machine guns, old tank turrets placed on concrete bases as well as minefields and barbed wire curtains. Hence, each battery formed a genuine little camp entrenched on the edge of the coast.

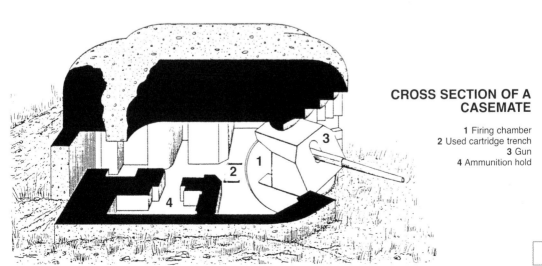

CROSS SECTION OF A CASEMATE

1 Firing chamber
2 Used cartridge trench
3 Gun
4 Ammunition hold

THE LONGUES-SUR-MER BATTERY

CROSS SECTION AND PLAN OF A CASEMATE

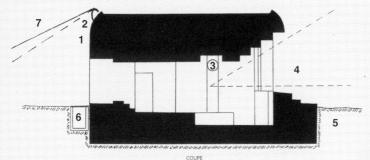

COUPE

1 Concrete roof
2 Hook for camouflage netting
3 Ventilation duct
4 Vertical firing range
5 Concrete foundation
6 Sump for streaming water evacuation
7 Camouflage netting

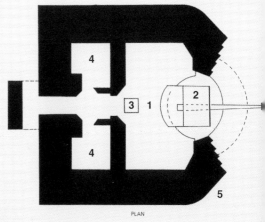

PLAN

1 Firing chamber
2 Gun
3 Trench
4 Ammunition hold
5 Abutment

PLAN OF THE BATTERY IN JUNE 1944

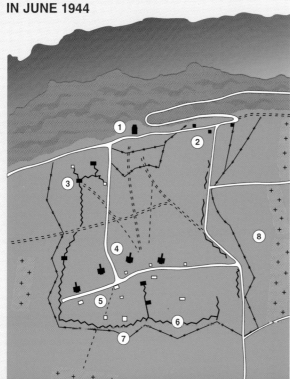

The four casemates can be distinguished with their gun, shelters, ammunition holds and, in the foreground, the firing command post. Each artillery position, surrounded by a minefield, constituted a strong point.

1 Firing command post
2 Tobruk or machine gun emplacement
3 Shelter and ammunition hold
4 Casemates
5 Ammunition holds
6 Trenches
7 Barbed wire
8 Mines

THE BATTERY COMMAND POST

Located 300 m in front of the casemates, on the brink of the cliff, the Longues battery's half-buried command post comprises two floors. On the ground floor were the observation post with a crenel (frontal gap) largely covering a 180 degree angle, the map room, a telephone exchange, and sleeping quarters for gunners. The upper floor housed, under a 70 cm thick concrete slab supported by four small steel posts, the telemetry post (optical device capable of determining the distance of a target). Once the target had been identified by the watchmen, using binoculars placed on a tripod, and the distance calculated by telemetry, the coordinates were transmitted by telephone to the artillery gunners. One of the most famous scenes of the film "The Longest Day" was shot in the Longues command post.

■ Firing command post.

■ Longues – the Firing command post and two casemates in the background.

23

THE LONGUES-SUR-MER BATTERY

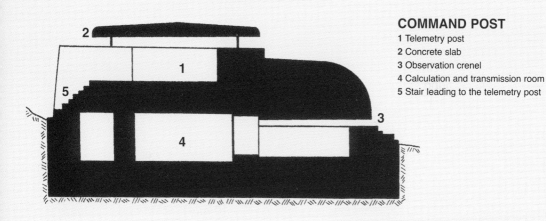

COMMAND POST
1 Telemetry post
2 Concrete slab
3 Observation crenel
4 Calculation and transmission room
5 Stair leading to the telemetry post

■ Longues – Rear view of the firing command post. Access to the telemetry post is via an embedded metal ladder, the same as those on warships.

AERIAL BOMBINGS

Located in the heart of the future landing zone, capable of firing at approaches not only on the future British assault position on Gold Beach (Asnelles) but also on

■ Gold Beach (Asnelles), the British assault position on the morning of the 6th of June. This moving picture shows the barges for the landing of troops and heavy vehicles. It was a British unit, landed on Gold Beach, that was to capture the Longues artillery battery on the morning of the 7th of June.

the American Omaha Beach (Colleville-Saint-Laurent), the Longues battery, equipped with modern German guns, needed to be neutralised before the 6th of June. With this in mind, the allied command decided to proceed to the aerial bombing of the artillery position throughout the weeks prior to the D-day landings. The most violent bombing took place between the 28th of May and the 3rd of June 1944. According to a German report, the battery had suffered some 1,500 bombs, some of them wei-

ghing 2,000 kg and capable of producing a crater 7 metres deep! Thanks to their 2 m thick ceiling and their concrete foundations, the casemates resisted to this avalanche of shells that essentially damaged the transmission lines buried between the command post and the firing blocks. On the night of the 5th to the 6th of June, between midnight and dawn, around 1,200 RAF heavy bombers set out to drop 6,000 tons of explosives on the 10 most incommodious batteries positioned along the future landing zone. At daybreak, 1,400 light and medium bombers from the US Air Force took over and attacked, for the second time in only a few hours, the same 10 batteries. Certain bombings were inaccurate due to heavy clouds, and the results were therefore somewhat irregular.

■ Allied bomber above the Normandy groveland.

However, one thing was certain; the artillery positions had been severely disjointed after the creation of several hundred craters, and the morale of the German garrison, barricaded up inside their blockhouses, had reached its lowest throughout the terrible deluge. The Longues battery was particularly dangerous, representing a hazard for approaches on both Gold and Omaha beaches, and was therefore a prime target, bombed by 124 allied planes unloading 600 tons of bombs, the same quantity that was dropped on Pointe du Hoc. Nevertheless, on the morning of the 6th of June 1944, the four guns remained intact.

Action plan for the Longues battery attack

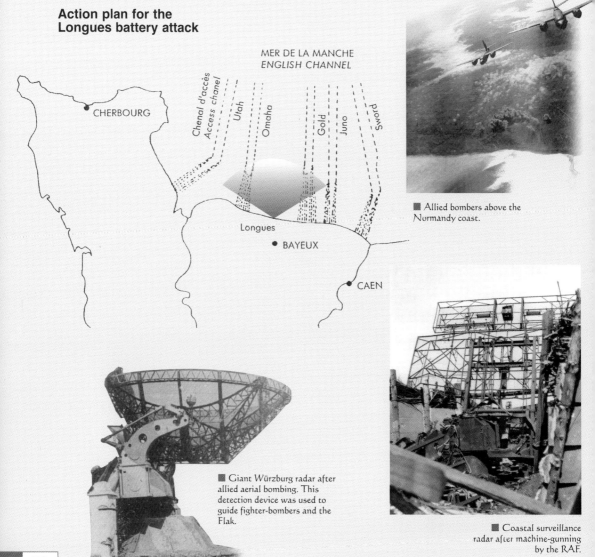

■ Allied bombers above the Normandy coast.

■ Giant Würzburg radar after allied aerial bombing. This detection device was used to guide fighter-bombers and the Flak.

■ Coastal surveillance radar after machine-gunning by the RAF.

NAVAL BOMBINGS AND GERMAN ARTILLERY GUNNER RETALIATION

After the aerial attacks, the action plan aimed at neutralising the German coastal guns, then provided for the naval artillery to enter into action. Thirty four cruisers and battleships and a hundred destroyers had therefore taken position, on the morning of the 6th of June, facing the Normandy shores. Firing began at daybreak, half an hour before the first troops set foot on French soil. By then, there was enough daylight for observers, in planes relentlessly circling above the batteries, to guide and adjust the firing coordinates of the huge naval artillery.

Here is an extract from the Swedish Colonel B. Stjernfelt's book entitled, "Alert on the Atlantic Wall" on the subject of the Longues battery.

■ Allied warship facing the Normandy coastline on the morning of the 6th of June 1944.

"The Longues battery was rapidly engaged in combat against the allied naval forces. It opened fire for the first time at 05h37, twenty minutes before sunrise. Ten sprays of water rose from the Channel close to the US Emmons destroyer. Furthermore, the battery targeted the battleship Arkansas that was busy firing to cover the Omaha sector. No less than 17 km separated the battery from its target. The battleship retaliated with twenty 305 mm shells and one hundred and ten 127 mm shells. The battery then ceased fire and pointed its guns eastwards. Closer targets had just come into its firing range. Landing in the British sectors was taking form and the command ship Bulolo, the flagship transporting the entire Staff of the Gold Beach troops, had just anchored at approximately 12,000 m from the coast facing Longues. At 5h57, the battery opened fire on its new target which was covered with huge bursts of sea-water and was obliged to withdraw seawards before being hit... the cruiser Ajax immediately came to the rescue. After an artillery duel at a distance of 11,000 metres, during which the cruiser fired one hundred and fourteen 150 mm shells, the Longues battery temporarily ceased firing at 6h20. When the landing operation began on Omaha beach, the battery resumed fire, showering the troops on the shoreline. Against Gold Beach, the battery entered rapidly into action and its gunfire was, apparently, efficient. However, because of the limited firing range of the artillery pieces surrounded by concrete, only those situated on the wings were able to precisely target the narrow strip of beach. Twice more, the Allies opened heavy artillery fire on the battery. Since the objective was to reduce the battery's artillery to silence as quickly as possible in order to avoid them causing disastrous losses among troops and material, the cruiser Argonaut came to assist the Ajax. When both ships had fired thirty-six 150 mm and twenty-nine 130 mm shells, the battery finally ceased fire. It was 8h45".

■■■ THE LONGUES-SUR-MER BATTERY

"This is only the British version of the combat between the Longues battery and the allied naval forces. In the same sector, there were the French cruisers Georges Leygues and Montcalm, attached to the Omaha Beach support sector, operating with the American battleship Arkansas.

The Georges Leygues was the first to open fire at 5h37 with a 152 mm shell (and not the Ajax as claimed by the official British report), soon to be followed by the Arkansas, which had a close shave, after which the two French cruisers continued firing. The German fire was to cease after retaliation from the Montcalm.

The battery resumed fire in the afternoon and it was only then that the Ajax, which belonged to the Gold sector support forces, entered into action. The French cruisers were engaged in combat against the battery shortly after 5 pm when the Ajax signalled to

Gunfire from the warships had caused considerable material damage. Of the four artillery pieces, three had been put out of combat. The British cruiser Ajax had fired with exceptional accuracy (thanks to radar), thus accomplishing an unquestionable stroke of genius. It had the highest percentage of successful fire of the entire naval artillery during the landing combat. The Swedish Colonel, a specialist of German artillery on the Atlantic Wall adds,

■ The General Eisenhower, in Normandy.

MAP SHOWING THE PLAN TO NEUTRALISE THE GERMAN COASTAL ARTILLERY BATTERIES

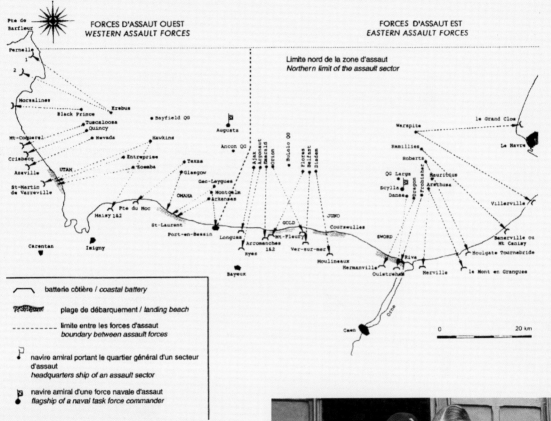

FORCES D'ASSAUT OUEST
WESTERN ASSAULT FORCES

FORCES D'ASSAUT EST
EASTERN ASSAULT FORCES

Limite nord de la zone d'assaut
Northern limit of the assault sector

batterie côtière / coastal battery

plage de débarquement / landing beach

limite entre les forces d'assaut
boundary between assault forces

navire amiral portant le quartier général d'un secteur d'assaut
headquarters ship of an assault sector

navire amiral d'une force navale d'assaut
flagship of a naval task force commander

0   20 km

them with a projector to cease fire against the Longues battery which was now her affair! The Georges Leygues, however, continued firing and pulled off two strikes on the fortification shortly before 7 pm.

As soon as it was possible to examine the debris on site, fragments carrying the unquestionable signature of French projectiles were found among the shrapnel." In short, both the French and the British claim victory.

■ Montgomery and the Overlord Flight Commander Leigh-Mallory, at the rear of the British Air Marshal's caravan.

THE SURRENDER OF THE LONGUES GARRISON

On the morning of the 7th of June, the Second Battalion Devonshire Regiment, from the 231st Infantry Brigade belonging to the 50th Northumbrian Division, which had landed on Gold Beach the previous day, was approaching the battery from the east. With its 200 gunners of an average age of 40 to 45 years, the Longues garrison surrendered to the British troops without resistance, contrary to those defending the Saint-Marcouf battery, located behind Utah Beach, who withstood the American assault until the 11th of June.

According to Stjernfelt, the Longue battery gunners' morale was at an all time low.

They reckoned that captivity was the most secure and the fastest way to put an end to the war. They hoped to be sent to America as prisoners.

■ Morning of the 6th of June, British troops landing on Gold Beach (Asnelles)

THE ATLANTIC WALL, A FUTILE FORTIFICATION?

■ Vasouy, near Honfleur. Casemate equipped with 15 cm guns defending the entrance to the Seine estuary.

Despite the immense scale of construction work, executed in record time on the European coastline, the German defence system's resistance to the attacks it suffered in Normandy in June 1944 was a major disappointment. In spite of this defeat, the defence of the Western European coastline did play a significant role in German operations and in the advancement of the conflict in general.

The protection offered by the fortification during the final confrontation with the Anglo-Americans was well below the German command's expectations. Far from complete and far from resembling a wall; in other words a continuous obstacle approximating a concrete barrage, the Atlantikwall was in fact a more or less regular succession of solidly fortified elements representing major ports and separated by extensive and insufficiently secured gaps. This huge site, still under construction and one

of the very bases of the German defence strategy in the West, was, in 1944, no more than a linear defence system, lacking in depth and whose military value was irregular from one location to another. Without wishing to neglect the danger it represented to assailants, the Wall was, first and foremost, a symbol of prestige and intimidation.

The defeat of the fortification was also largely due to the allied assault strategy. Judging that the shortest route to invade Germany from England was in the Pas-de-Calais region, and never, or at least too belatedly, having imagined that the allies would attempt a landing operation without entering major ports, the German command had quite logically concentrated its major defence positions between Dunkirk and Le Havre and had articulated its entire system around major ports, inevitable itineraries for assailants, or so they thought.

■ Two-floor firing command post at the German artillery position in Vasouy, twin sister to the Longues command post.

THE ATLANTIC WALL, A FUTILE FORTIFICATION?

By carrying out their amphibian attack between major ports, on exposed beaches and what's more, to the south rather than to the north of the Seine, the Allies were to brilliantly bypass a defence system that had not been designed to face such an eventuality. Via its somewhat unorthodox nature, the D-day operation was to throw the German command off balance and to paralyse its reflexes.

Despite its weaknesses and its defeat during the bombardment (the Wall was overcome before midday on the 6th of June on four beaches and, by evening on Omaha Beach) the fortification was not totally unprofitable to the Reich. The Atlantic Wall had, above all, obliged the Allies to give up any plans to land in the Pas-de-Calais where the German defensive organisation was at its strongest, hence abandoning highly superior strategic potential towards the Ruhr.

The coastal defence also obliged the Allies to undertake substantial preparatory manœuvres and to gather considerable resources which would not have been necessary had the coast been totally exposed.

In short, the Atlantic Wall represented a considerable hindrance to the general advancement of the conflict

■ Battle of Normandy. Wrecked German tank. To a greater extent than the Atlantic Wall which withstood the powerful Allied assault with only mediocre resistance, it was the German Army itself, exhausted after three years of war on the Russian front, that was overwhelmed in Normandy.

installed a DCA (anti-aircraft defence) post on the roof of the casemate and to have stored, inside, ammunition that exploded for some unknown reason. It was the violence of the explosion that caused the destruction of the concrete cube together with its gun, and not, as can often be read, a shot from allied naval artillery.

Located in the heart of the allied assault zone, between the American and the British landing beaches close to Arromanches, the Longues battery is one of the highpoints of the D-day landing circuit. The only battery to have preserved its guns, Longues not only bears witness to the last great fortification built by man, but is also a tangible example of the German occupation in our region and an excellent place of remembrance of the Second World war.

■ The staff bunkers were equipped with a periscope enabling the secure surveillance of the surroundings.

After the surrender of the German troops defending the Longues battery, the Royal Air Force engineers took control of the cliff-top and set up an airfield, known as B 11 and which was operational from the 26th of June to the 4th of September. This rural aerodrome, equipped with a 1,200 m landing strip covered with a square-linked metal grid, was to accommodate some fifty aircraft. According to certain witness reports, the aerodrome was responsible for the destruction of the fourth casemate to the east of the battery. In order to protect the B 11 airfield, the British are said to have

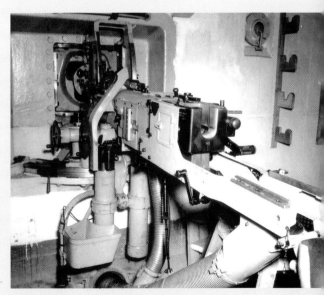

■ Interior of one of the Atlantic Wall's anti-tank gun casemates.

■ Panoramic view from the firing command post. The casemates are visible on the left.

■ Panoramic view to the west of the American sector of Omaha Beach and Point du Hoc.

■ There are approximately 70 metres between each casemate.

THE CLIFF

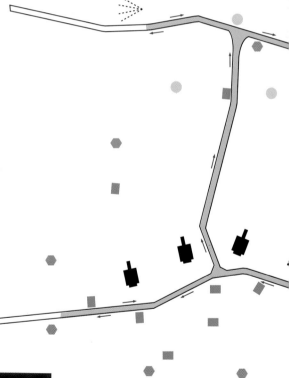

■ Next to the tourist office, this memorial is a reminder of the proximity of the B 11 airstrip at Longues-sur-Mer.

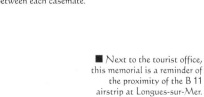

A 300 METRES A L'EST
SE TROUVAIT L'AERODROME
B 11 DE LONGUES SUR MER
OPERATIONNEL DU 21 JUIN 1944
AU 4 SEPTEMBRE 1944 AU COURS
DE CETTE PERIODE J. AUBERTIN
P. CLOSTERMANN ET J. REMLINGER
HEROS DES F.A.F.L SE TROUVAIENT
EN CE LIEU AU SEIN DU
SQUADRON 602 CITY OF GLASGOW
UNITES EGALEMENT PRESENTES
SQUADRON 132 CITY OF BOMBAY
SQUADRON 453 RAAF
SQUADRON 441 RCAF